Robert Greacen was born in Derry City in 1920. Over a poetic career spanning sixty years, he has produced six individual collections: *One Recent Evening* (1944), *The Undying Day* (1948), *A Garland for Captain Fox* (1975), *Young Mr. Gibbon* (1979), *Carnival at the River* (1990) and *Protestant Without A Horse* (1997). His *Collected Poems 1944-1994* (1995) won the Irish Times Literature Prize for Poetry. An autobiographical memoir, *Even Without Irene* (1969) has been updated and published under the title *The Sash My Father Wore* (1997). His most recent book is a collection of critical essays, *Rooted in Ulster: Nine Northern Writers* (2001).

LUNCH AT THE IVY

LUNCH AT THE IVY

ROBERT GREACEN

LAGAN PRESS
BELFAST
2002

The author would like to thank the editors of the following magazines in which some of these poems have appeared: *Acumen, Poetry Ireland Review, Books Ireland, Daily Express* and *Other Poetry.*

Published by
Lagan Press
183 University Avenue
Belfast BT7 1GZ

ISBN: 1 873687 92 3
Author: Greacen, Robert
Title: Lunch at the Ivy
2002

Set in Palatino
Printed by Noel Murphy Printing, Belfast

for Shirley Toulson—
in celebration of a long friendship

Old men ought to be explorers
Here and there does not matter
We must be still and still moving
Into another intensity ...
　　　　　　—T.S. Eliot, *East Coker*

CONTENTS

GOOD, BAD

Days good, days bad
Weeks good, weeks bad
Months good, months bad
Years good, years bad
Decades good, decades bad
Lifetimes good, lifetimes bad
Deaths good, deaths bad

CARTOGRAPHERS

Old men are cartographers.
We map the coloured countries
Our childhood dreamed of.
Down the corridors of years
We see the streets of freedom
Where pirates and cowboys roam;
The tram that clangs to Eden,
The ships heading for exotic ports:
Marseilles, Piraeus, St. Petersburg.
Lands and seas light up
As we lie in the dark,
Hopping from country to country.
Old men before and after sleep
Draw maps, hear distant voices.
River gods and Sirens sing us
To islands, deltas, archipelagos.

SHIPWRECK
for Rory Brennan

'Old age is shipwreck,'
Said a great Frenchman.*
The captain's past it
The crew have scurvy
The cook has jumped overboard.
The engine stalls
The compass lies.
Liners and yachts sail by
Intent on their own occasions
But blind to shipwreck.
Lost in dreams and memories
Old men cling to rafts,
Regretting, remembering,
Staring at a neutral sea.

* Charles de Gaulle

BLUE PLAQUES

X, the great composer, was born here.
Y, the Nobel physicist, died in this house.
Z, the famous poet, wrote here in his prime.
They all figure in reference books.
They all have been biographed.
They all got their blue plaques.
Their plaques are stared at by Yanks,
Immaculate Japanese click cameras at them,
Our countrymen simply walk by.
Ah Fame, that goddess they lusted after,
Where are they now, the Great and the Good?
Who reads Sir Walter or Alfred Lord Tennyson?
Who remembers Kelvin or Tom Moore
To whom Lord Byron drank a double health?
Yet, perhaps, a phrase or stanza remains,
Perhaps composer X's opera tune is hummed,
Perhaps ohm or watt or Celsius or Fahrenheit
To someone means men not measurements.
Perhaps blue plaques are not wholly daft.

Damn it, I think I'll settle for one myself.

CORKSCREW
in memory of Clifford Dyment (1914-1971)

Twist, twist, twist right through the cork,
Then clockwise turn slow, turn sure—
Out comes the cork clean as a lancet.
Clifford used that corkscrew constantly—
Since he died it has slaved for me.
I knew him best in his last phase,
Poet deserted by the Muse.
Once 'in' he ended 'out'.
I'd go to dinner at his flat
Two stone throws from Gloucester Road,
Climb his sky-high corkscrew stairs.
'Nothing to celebrate', Clifford would say,
Then a dramatic pause, a Cheshire smile:
'Anyway, my friend, let's celebrate.'
His corkscrew would be conscripted
In London then, as now by me in Dublin.
We'd celebrate in cheap Algerian plonk,
He'd talk of famous friends departed,
Of feckless Dylan, his fellow Welshman
Who once had snored on Clifford's couch.
Dinner over, our glasses brimmed,
He'd curse, then bless, the fickle Muse.

IN MEMORIAM JOHN MIDGLEY (1921-2000)

In the grey shadow of Cave Hill
Jack brimmed our glasses of Marsala.
Could it be less than a century ago?
Not that we remained grape loyalists
In the 'Crown', the 'Egg', the 'Welly Park'
Where Jack would quote from Louis,
Talk of a stint in India with the 'Skins',
Young Lieutenant Midgley in the Raj.
On Sundays I'd tramp with him and Aileen,
Watch him arm himself with branches
To build back home an eager fire
Before the vino was uncorked.
Of all the memories one holds fast:
That evening of homage to Marsala,
Sicily's gift to dour Belfast.

ALEX COMFORT, LONDONER (1920-2000)

The good fairies loaded him with gifts
Yet at sixteen science claimed four fingers
After an experiment, but left an active thumb.
A trip to Argentina followed, yielded
The Silver River, a travel book, in just two years.
Did that experiment turn Alex's heart against
The trade of arms, the brutal game of war
That he called murder, humanity's disgrace?
He looked on Dresden and Hiroshima as crimes,
Joined the aged Russell in A-bomb protests,
Was sentenced to a month as the nation's 'guest'.
Then he championed sex as therapeutic,
A way to gentle the male from violence.
Science, fiction, poetry, politics gave rise
To fifty books, a varied wordhoard.
He wrote his blockbuster, *The Joy of Sex*,
Not that it was his favourite work.
With Jane he flew to California,
Later returned to live in Kent:
Told me—'England's better for the old.'
Yet in my mind Alex is ever young.
Poems for Jane he sent me, inscribed:
'One survivor to another, 1986.'
I see him now the Cambridge prodigy
In corduroys, glove on his left hand,
Stunning me with talk, talk, talk,
Mapping out my literary career
As we worked on our anthology, *Lyra*.
'Keep writing, Bob', he counselled.
I see him in Dublin at the Rotunda,
He corrects me on de Valera's Constitution.
We ride together on a No. 10 to Donnybrook
(Dublin puts him in mind of Wisbech)
To argue in Reddin's with Cecil Salkeld,

Painter and local polymath.
Alex, a workaholic, issues a warning:
'Don't waste your time in pubs, Bob.'
Memory on memory—London, Dublin.
I still can hear that cataract of talk,
Sane doctor in a world gone mad.
How can I find words to honour him?

AT A LONDON CREMATORIUM

'Ah yes, he started well,
I'll grant you that.
Think of the risks he took,
The rocket drive of that first book.
But what about the long slow slide,
The language limp and flat?
Ah yes, my friend, he lost his touch
And what is even worse
The bastard wrote too much.'

KELLY

The Times obit. buried him in superlatives —
Lord Kelly, icon of the Establishment,
Lauded by the great and good, an authority
On osteomyelitis, a bigwig of medicine,
Hero of a thousand surgeries, adroit fixer.
All that and more, yet for me he's simply Jim,
A whey-faced lad, scorned by his schoolmates,
Jostled in the playground, a cornered boy.
A new master once, writing down our names,
Asked Jim to spell his out—
'K-E-double L-Y, James Kally.'
'Ah,' said the master, 'like the French town.'
Lickspittles, we sniggered in *schadenfreude*.
Years on, I heard that Jim was a doctor.
'You're joking—surely not Jim Kally?'
Upwards he soared: pundit in Harley Street,
Consulted by dukes and princes, people said,
A fluent advocate for his profession,
Then an M.P. for a Royal borough.
He scooped up a knighthood and a peerage.
Only the Order of Merit eluded him.
Not bad, not bad at all for our Jim Kally.

THE VISITOR

Prof. Wilson, Dr. Jackson, Mr. Kelly?
Call him also Schmidt, Dupont, Lopez.
Sometimes with moustache or beard
Or skin as smooth as glass,
He can seem Nordic, Greek, Chinese,
Act macho or like a gentleman,
Be boyish, jovial, grave, doddery.
To most eyes he is invisible.
In Savile Row and handmade shirt
Or tatty jacket, jeans near done
He steps from a taxi or fast car
Or just gets off a humble bike.
Bolts and threats won't keep him out
Nor frantic calls to the police.
When he comes with his faint smile
Some cry in terror to whatever god.
Be smart, be on the winning side,
Reach out, grip tight his hand.

HE/SHE

He's the world's top workaholic,
A round-the-clock guy, C-in-C
Of an army on red alert.
He holds the aces, wins every game.
Is he black or white or brown?
A yuppie, an oldster with a frown?
Or a closet 'she' and not a 'he'?
Your guess is as good as mine,
But we are both on his hit list
And no one outsmarts that swine.

ARDNAGASHEL

Freddy and I in Cork
Greeted the Mardyke
Of O'Connor and O Faolain,
Drank in the Imperial.
Cork lit up, Europe dark.
Went to Bantry by rail,
Cycled out to Ardnagashel
The six or seven miles
In-out that fissured coast,
Glossy postcard Ireland
Of 100,000 welcomes.
But shadowed Ireland:
Croziers ruling O.K.,
Censors at work
The vanishing Irish.
In recent memory
Peelers choked in blood
Big houses torched,
Drunk Black and Tans
On murder sprees,
Michael Collins towering
Over the rebel county
Then falling dead.
Now Europe burning,
Ireland dazed, inert,
And Belfast blitzed.
Freddy and I whistled
Bantered our way
To Ardnagashel House,
Ten or more bedrooms
Anglo yet untouched,
The Hutchins name respected.
That night I overheard
The gentle swagger

Of the Bay waters
Lulla-lulla-lulla
Hithering, dithering
Where once the warships
Flew St. George's Cross,
Their officers standing
Easy at Ardnagashel,
Drinking gin & tonic.
Patricia the chatelaine
Kissed me in the moonlight
At Ireland's Camelot.
I took her hand
Strode into the future.

TELLING THE DIFFERENCE
for Leslie Gillespie

That evening, after fooling around with pals,
I ate Billy's greasy concoction,
Then drank two glasses of whiskey.
At eighteen I said goodbye
To my lemonade youth.
Back home, my stomach turned,
I spilled the mess out in the kitchen.

I had expected scorn from the old man
But Dad proved kindly,
So I asked him to tell me
The difference between Scotch and Irish.

He provided a lesson
No schoolmaster had taught,
Not even Mr. Marshall who knew his claret.
I thought: In all my precious books
I couldn't have come across such expertise.
Could G.B.S. or Aldous Huxley
Tell Scotch from Irish?

Perhaps Dad thought:
This lad with his natty blazer,
Wide grey trousers like sails in the wind,
His posh-spoken friends,
May one day, God knows,
Turn into a man who can tell the difference.

THAT SUMMER

That summer the sky in Paris fell,
Marianne lay in the gutter, raped.
Ah yes, it was the worst of times
Yet at twenty years and sick at heart
Some days turned out the best of days.
Gillespie and I swanned all that summer,
The skin on my arms peeled in the sun,
The roads were dusty snake trails
That pulled us south to mild adventures.
Betrayed by time we dreamed at night,
Forsaken by our stars of destiny
But hopeful luck would see us right.
While Europe trembled in its martial dance
We laughed white days, dark nights away
And gave ourselves to life, to poetry.

LONDON 1936

It's 2000 AD as I peer
Through a wall of glass,
Gaze down a corridor
That runs to 1936.
Who is that lad?
Could it be my young self?
He gets off a train in Paddington,
Walks through Sunday-suited London,
Has his first glimpse of the capital,
Solid, unshakeable London—
Bayswater Road every inch bourgeois,
Marble Arch a hymn to Empire.
At Speakers' Corner he comes across
The talk-as-you-please orators
Flanked by grinning bobbies
With red faces, heavy boots.
Voices headline the air:
FREEDOM FOR INDIA!
END IRISH PARTITION!
ON GUARD FOR SPAIN!
VICTORY TO THE WORKERS!
He wanders on and on and on:
Big Ben, Buck House, the Strand,
Fleet Street, Ludgate Circus.
As he roams the imperial streets
Can I hear him murmur
'Sweet Thames! run softly
Till I end my song'?

LONDON, W8

A river of moonlight
Flooded the room
Where they touch-talked
Drank wine, played records
Until near midnight
When she led him
Up to the narrow room.
He stared out at
The moon, the moon, the moon
Lighting the square,
Listened to the pulse
Of body-beat, traffic,
Knocked and entered.
Walking home he knew
He would always remember
That square in Kensington,
The moon, the moon, the moon.

LUNCH AT THE IVY

An invitation to lunch—and at the Ivy!
I spent ten nail-biting minutes
Before he bounced in, Savile Row smart,
In his early fifties still London's pride.
"What will you drink?' he asked.
'Er, a dry sherry,' I replied, assuming nonchalance.
'Not very enterprising —how about vodka?'
He hissed in his crystal accent.
I watched him swoop on an ageing actress:
'How marvellous to see you dahling.
You were simply wonderful last night.'
He acted out his anecdotes,
An entertainer waiting for the laugh,
Brimful of failsafe wit and charm.
'Come back to the rehearsal with me.'
On the First Night I climbed the stairs
To the Haymarket eyrie at the top.
I shyly knocked and waited.
'Come in, dear boy, come in.'
'You were simply wonderful tonight,' I said.
He squeezed my hand until it hurt.
Later I nerved myself to write the book
I'd call 'The Art of Noël Coward.'

AT NUMBER 24

Ah, did I once see Eliot plain?
Well, yes, I did in 1949
In London's Russell Square
And if it matters, Number 24.
There the St. Louis eagle spread his wings,
A middle-aged future Nobel man.
He talked of poems for an anthology
(Of which I was co-editor)
That F & F would shortly publish.
I observed the features of clerical cut
That he himself had noted.
How pleasant to nod to *If* and *Perhaps* and *But*,
To hear the organ tones of that slow voice.
How delightful to meet Ezra's Old Possum
And see that mouth both open and shut.
Ah yes, I once saw T.S. Eliot plain.

'TAXI!'

She wrote the number on a used envelope.
'Give me a ring sometime, Robert.'
She'd been to visit Patricia and me,
Had brought along a bottle of claret
To our corner house in Church Walk
Where Ezra Pound once had a room triangular,
Harangued the young Robert Frost,
Was maddened by the bells of St. Mary Abbots.
She and I walked past Stone's bookshop,
Turned right and along Holland Street.
In Church Street I shouted 'Taxi!'
She was moving up fame's escalator,
Making friends with the opinion-formers
So 'Give me a ring sometime, Robert'
Sounded great—and yet and yet ...
I never made that call nor wrote
To give my reason why.
The future Dame was driven away
In her prime like Miss Jean Brodie.

SHADOWS

'In any case life is but a procession of shadows, and God knows
why it is that we embrace them so eagerly, and see them depart
with such anguish being shadows.'

—Virginia Woolf, *Jacob's Room*

The shadows turn away. Who is that man,
A prisoner of mislaid hopes, who shuffles in distress,
Through the moraine of the years? What soul unblessed?
The coming was hard, but touching the liquid fire was harder,
Down, down, down into the shifting nightmare depths,
Falling through forests green and spongy where a thousand
            metallic eyes
Glinted from snakeheads like a thousand little fires.
Look up, first shadow, and see the zigzag way you came!
(He cannot lift his head for shame.) O the way was long,
The coming was hard and soft by fits and starts,
As he fell and twisted but never resisted
And came in a dazzle and haze of amazement.
But look! the second shadow is stippled
With startling brightness, as though pinpointed by vivid day
—His twin lies passionless, mute, mantled in night—
For he resisted falling, all the way.
True, he also fell in the end, witness his wounds.
He turns his head towards the broken back of the sky,
And seemingly finds pearce in this outlaw sphere of loneliness,
Knows freedom through necessity, finds life in death.

1954

FIRST MEETING

I caught her glance across the room,
A face etched on an ancient coin
While on the rug Dolores sprawled
Her head loyal between my knees.
I touched the raven Latin hair
Swam in the dark eye pools.

Patricia blonde, a Nordic queen,
Surveyed the guests with regal air,
Talked of her years in France
In Madame de Forceville's château
Before the Nazi panzers came.

How had I stumbled on such worlds
Aeons from provincial innocence?
Which might I try to enter
Or perhaps be chosen for?
Dark or fair, of ice or fire?

Patricia smiled across the room
When tying on her fur-trimmed hood,
Then vanished into night and light.

Did something in me die?
Was there a hint of birth?

THE STRANGER

The bell shrilled in the winter hall.
'That'll be Patricia,' said her friend.
He ran down the stairs from the party
To greet this stranger he'd heard of.

She wore a kind of fur-trimmed hood,
Stood tall on the outside step
Of a Georgian house in Raglan Road,
A daughter of the Anglo-Irishry.

Now, after fifty years or more,
That picture flashes on a screen:
A youth in tweed jacket and corduroys,
The girl in the fur-trimmed hood.

She smiles and he smiles back.
'Yes, I'm Patricia,' she says.

SHOES IN OXFORD STREET

A kitten-heel slingback (two tone),
That's what Adam gave Eve.
Shoes trimmed with a bow,
Made to a hole-punch design.
'Eden's apples be blowed',
Said Eve to Adam—
'Those shoes are simply divine.'

VARENGEVILLE

If Patricia were still alive
She'd tease out my memories,
Not that I've quite forgotten
Our holiday in Varengeville.
A Frenchman drove us there
With Gallic panache.
We hurtled through Normandy
As if we were off to rescue
The saintly Joan of Arc
From the English goddams.
I played the glouton,
Later punished by a boil
Back in grey London.
We had a second honeymoon
Our love sky-blue
Yet our joy was tarnished.
'C'est un chien,' the driver said
As he dragged the body away.
Patricia and I were upset
As we hurtled on through France,
Poplar after poplar after poplar,
To confort moderne in Varengeville.
It was only a dog after all
Yet its death somehow mattered.

SEVEN CATS
for John Heath-Stubbs

The parson's cat is a pious cat
In the church he caught a rat.

The doctor's cat is a healthy cat,
Not too lean, not too fat.

The lawyer's cat is a solemn cat,
Sober as a judge he often sat.

The sportsman's cat's an active cat,
Likes to play with ball and bat.

The scholar's cat is a serious cat
Who sits and ponders on a mat.

The lady's cat is a pampered cat,
Enjoys his gin and a cosy chat.

The poet's cat is a rhyming cat,
Rat, fat, sat, bat, mat, chat.

ONCE UPON A CHRISTMAS

Once upon a Christmas and all the golden bells
ding-donging Bethlehem and the risefall of voices
and the trills of laughter deep in my heart's well trembling
upwards and soundlessly spilling out
over the rooftops and snow on the Christmas cards
and Father Christmas dizzy with chimney errands
and small 'f' father swilling Guinness like a
nippling baby lost in a rainbow haze of betting
windfalls then wiping moustache on navy serge
sleeve and mother bustling and singing Christians Awake!
salute the morn of mornings the day of Christbirth that was
dark and gloomy just like the
others but oh electric fingers on tinselled parcels
and tense teeth snapping through plump flesh of
goose and throat a-gargling in lemonade with champagne
bubbles at the brim and feeling fit to
burst and afternoon heavy as putty and father
stupefied on the shiny horsehair sofa and evening
of cold ham and tinned pineapple-chunks and mother
reading *A Christmas Carol* oh isn't it luvly she
says no one will ever write like Charles Dickens
again no not if I live till a hundred and Dickens bookcased
and cocoa drunk up the squeaking stairs
and at last alone in the darkness listening to
steel-tipped heels cracking the frosty pavements
and sheepcounting ninety-nine a hundred a hundred and
one two three oh in the darkness Christmas
please never never end while the golden bells
ding-dong to Bethlehem and back again in
candlelight once upon once upon a Christmas deep
as dreamland cosy as a feather bed deep deep deep
once upon a Christmas.

NEIGHBOURS
for Seamus Heaney

In your birth-year I bought a Remington,
Shyly tapped out romantic verse,
Runes against the lightless nights,
The warplanes in our northern sky.

By odd conspiracy and chance
Five decades on, we are neighbours,
Each anchored in Yeats' Sandymount,
Both servants of the craft and mystery.

REMEMBERING ADLESTROP
for Shirley Toulson

I, too, remember Adlestrop
Because one Sunday moming
A friend and I drove there—
Yes, it was late June.
We saw the railway nameplate
That Edward Thomas saw
Through the train window.
No one came and no one left
While we were strolling round.
There were cloudlets in the sky.
We heard no blackbird's song.
In Oxfordshire and Gloucestershire
The birds made not a chirp
Yet they sang for Edward Thomas.

L'HOMMAGE À GEORGES SIMENON

Danger ahead, violent ends, a sense of guilt.
At the inquest on Bouvet the stowaway
He gets a new lease of life on the iron staircase.

Then, in the blue room Monsieur Monde vanishes.
The disappearance of Odile in the Venice train
Is solved by the couple from Poitiers and Uncle Charles.

The outlaw, after the long exile, writes his intimate memoirs.
The girl in his past never forgets her four days in a lifetime,
Finds solace at the bottom of a bottle with an African trio.

The rich man imprisons the cat in a glass cage
Yet provides a teddy bear for the little saint,
Enjoys striptease, greets the man from Archangel.

Monsieur X frequents the gardens of the crematorium.
'C' etait un homme merveilleux, mais combien difficile!'
Said Denyse twenty-one years after his death.

ECSTASY

At school the only word I stumbled over
Was 'ecstasy', by making that second 's' a 'c'.
Mr. Marshall ringed the mistake in red.

Later I came across the word in French.
L'extase, with 's' of course, meant sex and sin.
Mon dieu, the bloody word was feminine.
We schoolboys sniggered over 'vocabulaire':
'Maîtresse', 'putain', 'pissoir'.
The French, it seemed, were far from nice.

Now in The Times, no less, I read:
PROOF THAT ECSTASY DAMAGES THE BRAIN.
Damage, it's said, to thought, emotion, memory,
According to the whitecoat boys in Baltimore.

How sad I am to know, long out of school
That spell it as you may, the Puritans
Were right to take the view
That ecstasy (or almost anything you crave,
Like cigarettes or gin or certain kinds of sex)
Is very, very bad for you.

CRASH!

A smiling winter day, sun-sprinkled,
Roads flaunt their dry-bone arms,
The engine croons, the city lights
Shepherd us home to dusk and wine
Yet time and chance must rule.
The driver glances down,
Fumbles the wheel, swerves
Right into a bollard.
Crash! crash! crash!
I lie hours-long on a trolley,
The driver, air-bag saved, sits by me,
Mumbles a litany of guilt.
'Shut up!' I shout, 'Just bloody carelessness!
Blame fate, the gods, but not yourself!'
Days pass, I walk the corridors of pain,
Inhabit depression's dim-lit cell,
Snatch at life on the telephone.
Before I sleep I turn and turn,
Questions flood through my mind:
Will there be daffodils this spring?
Will roses scent. the summer air?
Will this? Will that ...?
I freefall into black dreams.

KINSKY'S RETURN TO LONDON

Remember Kinsky—and his flight to Ankara
And how he gave us all the slip?
I got his cryptic postcard:
'Great is Diana of the Ephesians. K.'
Was this in code or what?
Where was he? In a Turkish prison
Tortured, half-starved, this Kurdish Jew?
Rumours spiralled for years.
Some said he had holed up in Eilat,
There tapping out a novel in Hebrew.
Others thought him a dead statistic,
Remembered only by a knot of friends.

One midnight; the telephone shrilled.
'It's Kinsky. In London. I'm back.
See you at the old place tomorrow,
Eight of the evening clock.
No, no. No time for talk.
Ears everywhere, my friend, Shalom.'

A plane to Heathrow,
A taxi spattering its way east
Over the laminated roads
Past the pubs and clubs
Of leafy Holland Park Avenue,
The Bayswater Road, Park Lane.

Carrington-Smythe awaited me,
Called for double scotches,
Charmed me as ever
With anecdotes of Captain Fox.
We waited, drank, waited, drank,
Yet even at 10 p.m. no arrival.

A waiter ushered in a London bobby,
Respectful, helmet under his arm.
Bad news. Kinsky gunned down in the Strand,
His briefcase snatched away.
Yes, instant death. The Special Branch
Fingerprinting, probing, arresting.
Carrington-Smythe swam before my eyes,
I spilled the scotch over my trousers.

THE FIXER

Some say there never was a Captain Fox.
Well, then I'll call a witness:
One Derek Stanford, poet, sage,
A citizen of London and the world.
He'll swear on any Bible you can find
That he saw Fox as plain could be
In Brighton town with Lord Olivier,
Actors both and men of action too.
He caught some words of Fox:
'Larry, the PM's in a right old tizz.
I told him I could fix it.'
'Quite so', said Lord Olivier,
'You're just the man, old chap.'
They talked a while, these Thespians,
Then laughed, embraced like Latins,
Parted, their business despatched.
Stanford watched their ego-dance,
Knowing he lived in interesting times.

LUCK

'Is he lucky?' Napoleon asked
Before he promoted an officer.
So when there's a penalty shoot-out
To decide on win or lose,
Don't be tense or cock-a-hoop.
Be laid back, take it easy.

Go for it—net the ball.

LINES AFTER WILLIAM MCGONAGALL

When you are made miserable
By the cold wintry blast
In places as widely apart as
Toronto, Moscow and Belfast,
You must remember that in three
Or four months' time
A higher temperature will ensure
A reasonably tolerable clime.
Nevertheless, nobody but God can
Foretell the precise date
When the unpredictable winter
Will finally abate,
Thus bringing to all and sundry
The much desired spring
About which ninety per cent of
Poets and birds sing.

William McGonagall (1825 or 1830-1902): '... he now enjoys
a reputation as the world's worst poet.'
            —*Oxford Companion to English Literature* (1985)

THUNDERSTORMS

As if I'd pointed Uncle George's gun
The sheepdog cowered under the table.
God's moving his furniture, they said.
The Ulster air charged with electrons
Flashed and flushed to strike me dead
For I had stolen a biscuit from a tin.

Years after, at something like sixteen,
I stood upright beside my Uncle Jack
On his couth English lawn,
I watched him laugh at flash and fury
As the rain doused clean our heads
Freemason man and questing youth
Until a rainbow blessed us both.

FOLLOWING DARKNESS

Why burn with rage at close of day
Or act ungently as we turn to clay?
Fine rhetoric can win the heart
But does not comfort those who must depart.
Better to smile at fate, then coast along,
Hoping to follow darkness into song.

POETRY
from
LAGAN PRESS

Author: **Jean BLEAKNEY**
Title: *The Ripple Tank Experiment*
ISBN: 1 873687 52 4
Price: £5.95
No. of Pages: 72pp
Date of Publication: 1999

Debut collection from Belfast-based poet.

Author: **C.L. DALLAT**
Title: *Morning Star*
ISBN: 1 873687 47 8
Price: £4.95
No. of Pages: 88pp
Date of Publication: 1998

Debut collection from North Antrim poet and critic.

Author: **Moyra DONALDSON**
Title: *Snakeskin Stilettos*
ISBN: 1 873687 25 7
Price: £5.95
No. of Pages: 80pp
Date of Publication: 1998

Debut collection from Newtownards poet.

Author: **Moyra DONALDSON**
Title: *Beneath the Ice*
ISBN: 1 873687 69 0
Price: £5.95   **NEW**
No. of Pages: 72pp
Date of Publication: 2002

Second collection of poems from the Newtownards poet.

Author: **Norman DUGDALE**
Title: *Collected Poems 1970-1995*
with critical introduction by Philip Hobsbaum
& personal appreciation by Elizabeth Thomas
ISBN: 1 873687 45 1
Price: £6.95
No. of Pages: 194pp
Date of Publication: 1997

Collected poems of neglected northern poet. Includes
unpublished volume completed shortly before the poet's death.

Author: **James ELLIS**
Title: *Domestic Flight*
ISBN: 1 873687 30 3
Price: £6.95
No. of Pages: 128pp
Date of Publiction: 1998

Debut collection from well-known local actor.

Author: **Padraic FIACC**
Title: *Red Earth*
ISBN: 1 873687 90 7
Price: £4.95
No. of Pages: 64pp
Date of Publication: 1996

Collection based on Irish mythology from one of the north of
Ireland's leading poets.

Author: **Padraic FIACC**
Title: *Semper Vacare*
ISBN: 1 873687 43 5
Price: £5.95
No. of Pages: 72pp
Date of Publication: 1999

Collection from major Ulster poet, Sempre Vacare gathers
poems written over the last decade.

Author: **Sam GARDINER**
Title: *Protestant Windows*
ISBN: 1 873687 32 X
Price: £5.95
No. of Pages: 64pp
Date of Publication: 2000

Debut collection from the Portadown-born poet. Winner of the National Poetry Competition (1993).

Author: **Robert GREACEN**
Title: *Collected Poems 1944-1994*
with an preface by the author
ISBN: 1 873687 55 9
Price: £5.95
No. of Pages: 176pp
Date of Publication: 1995

Collected poems of the Belfast-born and Dublin-based poet. Winner of the Irish Times Award for Poetry 1995.

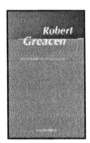

Author: **Robert GREACEN**
Title: *Protestant Without a Horse*
ISBN: 1 873687 37 0
Price: £5.95
No. of Pages: 72pp
Date of Publication: 1997

Collection from leading Ulster poet.

Author: **Sam HARRISON**
Title: *The Birds Fly Over*
Selected Poems
ISBN: 1 873687 31 1
Price: £4.95
No. of Pages: 80pp
Date of Publication: 1996

The selected poems of Belfast-born poet, The Birds Fly Over is the first ever gathering by the unjustly neglected poet.

Author: **Tess HURSON**
Title: *Vivarium*
ISBN: 1 873687 36 2
Price: £5.95
No. of Pages: 72pp
Date of Publication: 1997

Debut collection from Co. Tyrone poet.

Author: **Fred JOHNSTON**
Title: *Being Anywhere*
New & Selected Poems
with an introduction by the author
ISBN: 1 873687 63 X
Price: £6.95   **NEW**
No. of Pages: 112pp
Date of Publication: 2002

Selected by the Belfast-born poet this collection features the best of his previous six volumes as well as previously unpublished poems.

Author: **Richard KELL**
Title: *Collected Poems 1962-1993*
introduced by Fred Johnston
with a preface by the author
ISBN: 1 873687 12 5
Price: £7.95   **NEW**
No. of Pages: 248pp
Date of Publication: 2002

Definitive edition of the Cork-born poet's output. Features critical introduction by Fred Johnston.

Author: **Leon McAULEY**
Title: *Veronica*
ISBN: 1 873687 05 2
Price: £4.95
No. of Pages: 80pp
Date of Publication: 1994

Debut collection from North Antrim poet and children's writer

Author: **Roy McFADDEN**
Title: *Collected Poems 1943-1995*
with an introduction by Philip Hobsbaum
and preface and notes by the author
ISBN: 1 873687 16 8
Price: £7.95
No. of Pages: 382pp
Date of Publication: 1996

Collected poems of leading Northern Irish poet. Features
critical introduction by the founder of the Northern 'Group'
of poets, Philip Hobsbaum as well as preface and extensive
notes by the poet.

Author: **Hugh MAXTON**
Title: *Gubu Roi*
ISBN: 1 873687 62 1
Price: £6.95
No. of Pages: 92pp
Date of Publication: 2000

Collected satirical poems of the 1990s from leading Irish poet
and critic.

Author: **Pól Ó MUIRÍ**
Title: *D-Day*
ISBN: 1 873687 85 0
Price: £4.95
No. of Pages: 70pp
Date of Publication: 1995

English-language debut collection of Belfast-born Irish
language poet and short story writer.

Author: **Cherry SMYTH**
Title: *When the Lights Go Up*
ISBN: 1 873687 48 6
Price: £6.95
No. of Pages: 56pp
Date of Publication: 2001

Debut collection from Portrush-born poet.

Author: **Damian SMYTH**
Title: *Downpatrick Races*
ISBN: 1 873687 87 7
Price: £6.95
No. of Pages: 64pp
Date of Publication: 2000

Debut collection from Downpatrick-born poet and critic.

Author: **Andy WHITE**
Title: *The Music of What Happens*
ISBN: 1 873687 86 9
Price: £7.95
No. of Pages: 90pp
Date of Publication: 1998

Poems and song lyrics from leading Ulster singer-songwriter.

All titles can be ordered direct from:
Lagan Press, 138 University Avenue, Belfast BT7 5GZ
(Post and packing free)